WOMEN
ARE CROCKPOTS ROCKETS
MEN
ARE MICROWAVES AIRFYERS

ROCHELLE KELLY

ISBN: 978-1-965679-96-8 (sc)
ISBN: 978-1-965679-97-5 (e)

Rev. date: 03/03/2025

This is to my husband Carl L. Kelly jr. the family that we created by coming together

We were both married in St. Luke UMC this publication book is a testament of how his love show action in his living .

Don't Bring That Microwave Into The Bedroom

[Include any grant/funding information and a complete correspondence address.]

This where we find johnny/Lisa in matrimony having some minor intimacy moment concerns.{sex in the bedroom }

The strategies for both

1. Position self to hear from God (your own personal quiet time Whatever I am doing or look like it is an pledge to hear the voice of God that we have to be any thing other than a son or daughter you\God you gave me a love latter coming to a love laterinlife (the bible climb upon the watch tower
2. Ponder it check the of the word Love or meaning of words not trying to be clever language Love is going on with you
3. The silent but quite time looks with both{man woman)} doing the worship to in same area suggestions; 1. Hold each other softly not looking at each other then let the woman talk in a whisper voice (no loud voice }tell him what is going on with her. Put a 3 min.-8min. time limit at the beginning. After that he does the same he holds her close or hands and tell her what's going with him. 2. Each person man, woman in the same room put your

arms around you self resight Romans 8;28 and we know that God causes all things to work together for good to those who are called according to his purpose, looking at each other (calming down inside their self then let the conversation begin if one needs more time voice that to the other person

4. Pull out the Biblical Principles of the way GOD has set for marriage between a man, woman

Reading about the amorites or the jebusites you ask yourself what does this have to do with my life you are find this character of God{what sovenity of Holy spirit Jesus moreover as a married couple loving each other a man and woman

The Love Languages

Receiving GIFTS>thouhtfulmess makes people feellike a prioriaty and special

Quality Time >Uninterupted undivided attention show someone you care Engaging in

Important conversations

Acts of service > Let me help you, Broken commitments shows someone that they don't matter.

Physical Touch>nonverbal use of body and touch to show love connection and excitement

Words of Affrimation > verbal compliments that express love and appreciation

I Love You

Pose the Question

This where spitual principle Have I forgiven, ask yourself the question have I committed to that tithe m have I been still or have I tried it on my own .then the holy Spirit will start answering .

5 Plan obedience and Pin down a date

[Add Title Here, up to 12 Words, on One to Two Lines]

[The body of your paper uses a half-inch first line indent and is double-spaced. APA style provides for up to five heading levels, shown in the paragraphs that follow. Note that the word *Introduction* should not be used as an initial heading, as it's assumed that your paper begins with an introduction.]

Abstract

[The abstract should be one paragraph of between 150 and 250 words. It is not indented. Section titles, such as the word *Abstract* above, are not considered headings so they don't use bold heading format. Instead, use the Section Title style. This style automatically starts your section on a new page, so you don't have to add page breaks. (To see your document with pagination, on the View tab, click Reading View.) Note that all text styles for this template are available on the Home tab of the ribbon, in the Styles gallery.]

Keywords: [Add keywords here. To replace this (or any) tip text with your own, just select it and then start typing. Don't include space to the right or left of the characters in your selection.]

[Heading 1]

[The first two heading levels get their own paragraph, as shown here. Headings 3, 4, and 5 are run-in headings used at the beginning of the paragraph.]

[Heading 2][1]

[For APA formatting requirements, it's easy to just type your own footnote references and notes. To format a footnote reference, select the number and then, on the Home tab, in the Styles gallery, click Footnote Reference.]

[Heading 3].

[Include a period at the end of a run-in heading. Note that you can include consecutive paragraphs with their own headings, where appropriate.]

[Heading 4].

[When using headings, don't skip levels. If you need a heading 3, 4, or 5 with no text following it before the next heading, just add a period at the end of the heading and then start a new paragraph for the subheading and its text.] (Last Name, Year)

[Heading 5].

[Like all sections of your paper, references start on their own page, as you see on the page that follows. Just type in-text citations as you do any text of your paper, as shown at the end of this paragraph and the preceding paragraph.] (Last Name, Year)

[To see this document with all layout and formatting, such as hanging indents, on the View tab of the ribbon, click Reading View.]

References

Last Name, F. M. (Year). Article Title. *Journal Title*, Pages From - To.

Last Name, F. M. (Year). *Book Title.* City Name: Publisher Name

Footnotes

[1][Add footnotes, if any, on their own page following references. The body of a footnote, such as this example, uses the Normal text style. *(Note: If you delete this sample footnote, don't forget to delete its in-text reference as well. That's at the end of the sample Heading 2 paragraph on the first page of body content in this template.)*]

Tables

Table 1

[Table Title]

Column Head	Column Head	Column Head	Column Head	Column Head
Row Head	123	123	123	123
Row Head	456	456	456	456
Row Head	789	789	789	789
Row Head	123	123	123	123
Row Head	456	456	456	456
Row Head	789	789	789	789

Note: [Place all tables for your paper in a tables section, following references (and, if applicable, footnotes). Start a new page for each table, include a table number and table title for each, as shown on this page. All explanatory text appears in a table note that follows the table, such as this one. Use the Table/Figure style, available on the Home tab, in the Styles gallery, to get the spacing between table and note. Tables in APA format can use single or 1.5 line spacing. Include a heading for every row and column, even if the content seems obvious. A table style has been setup for this template that fits APA guidelines. To insert a table, on the Insert tab, click Table.]

Figures

Figure 1. [Include all figures in their own section, following references (and footnotes and tables, if applicable). Include a numbered caption for each figure. Use the Table/Figure style for easy spacing between figure and caption.]

For more information about all elements of APA formatting, please consult the *APA Style Manual, 6th Edition.*

This is when getting over the doormat effect. Keep mind this is after my husband had expired.

This was my time to mature in my faith. I'd had several attempted at getting independent in business.

So to take are of my family, used funds (money) that I received from a life insurance policy. Everyone saw me coming taking from me while I was giving trying to receive information to exceed expectations.

Attempting to be come an insurance agent, financial planner, jewelry sale person, Amazonian marketer, real state agent. Looking at those situations, the only sustaining factor was my believe that something greater than myself could carry me through this. Attending online courses to make sure staying updated with the technology part of the whole process During this test in my life having both children in universities , sustaining a positive attitude while motivating my children to stay in their programs.

A righteous man has many troubles, but lord delivers him from them all Psalams 34:19 (NIV)

The only true relationship in my believe and praying daily. Trusting in people at time not realizing yet that they had good intentions none really for what I was going through at that time. My children was hurting and I was hurting ask for help that no one was hearing failing because of the liars, cheater, greedy, jealous people surrounding me. Listen not realizing I was that calling myself trying to buy something that no one could sale or give me. Some of this was self inflicted due to my naïve thinking my faith was maturing. It was emotional pain beyond comparison of my previous experiences in this life.

Scriptures: John 16:33KJV These things I have spoken unto you, that is me might have peace, In the world ye have tribulation: but be of good cheer :I have overcome the world.

My interpretation was and is let your faith raise and be of courage I am (GOD)is with you.

With no one to trust now and my children gaining their independence from me. That I did want them to gain prosperity with less pain this was my thinking wrong . my children had to have some pain that gave them a closeness to the relationship with God through faith that I was experience at my older age. Hopeful that they get it young so it would not be the insurmountable pain I was going through this season in my life.

Scripture: Jeremiah 29:11 (KJV For I know the thoughts that I think toward you. Says the lord thoughts Of peace and not evil, to give you a future and a hope. Then you will call upon me and go and pray to me and I will listen to you.

God's Action Plan for your Life "T.D. Jakes wrote the following a place called there :

It doesn't matter where 'there' is for it matter you achieve you achieve soul satisfaction.

It matters that you attain your full purpose and potential.it matters that you attain your highest and best YOU.

Fastest lion , If he can not , he will be eaten. Every morning in Africa the lion awakens he onlyhas one thing on his mind to out run the slowest gazelle if not he will die of hunger. Whther yoi re chosen to be a Gazelle or a lion is of no consequence.it is enough to know that with the rising of the sun, yo must run futher than you did yesterday or you will die . This is the race of life. Batterson, Mark :\; CHASE A LION ON A SNOWNY DAY

Redundancy Worthy

The repetition in of life can be an indicator of a lesson not completely received.

The person whether a man or women gets caught up in trying to stay in perfection that at this time does not matter anymore.

Spaghetti Head Incident

This is the situation when a women is a croquet pot and men are microwaves in an example the child of both the wife and husband on this particular day. The child has a cold child had to be left at home with the babysitter. The husband { man) goes to work as usually do his work all day. The wife(woman] she goes to work call at least three times to check on their child. While husband has went about his day thinking departmentally that she is checking on the child so why should I do that. The wife is thinking what I am going to cook while continuing doing her daily work at the office. The husband is thinking the husband is thinking maybe I will meet my friends at the bar for a drink after work. The wife get home after being concerned about their child checks on child began dinner Husband ome in after work and gets a drink . when then he comes in shes been attending to their child exhausted he ask her what's for dinner ? she saids it in the kitchen listen you need to see about our child now because I have to prepare for tomorrow and rest he said I "ve got to have dinner while preparing for tomorrow she saids when aregoing to findout o see about our child did ou call once today to check on our child how our child was doing? That they both gointo a augumentative discussion that may or may not may be resolved with both coming to take give each other turn in the conversation to find out what each other needs in these incident with their lives.

Strategies In This Incident

1. Both need to call each other periodically during the day/ night .
2. Communicate during the day when child is not home sick/ill
3. Encourage each other with their job incidents when glitches happen at work
4. Pray with each other during the day/night about child and other incidents
5. Continue to consult with godly peers throughout marriage .

The Hearts of fracture relationships

This went the being as one will be developed he/she evocable circumstances

Their both birth their dreams. they were out in the a place of heavenly atmosphere nevertheless we both want/need embarked on our destination oberserving the many selection we had gathering presents abide loving on continue journey she/he challenging each other not sure yet whom presents while went in Various stores , entertainments, eatery, Disney ,Barnes and Nobles

While moving around they were having augmentative discussion nothing physical causes pains to each other then tomorrow

 Furthermore. he/she being intimacy with mediation in constant motion spending time with each other.

The Persevance Stradegy Of Their Togetherness

1. Stay in with our godly counselor us peers directing
2. A argumentative discussion define boundary
3. Perservance in continuous motion during perfect

The affirmation of …you unselfish also bitterness with anger

No longer not pleasing myself some in the challenge

No longer to be in unhealthy relationship

No longer holding grudges

No longer pity those with challenges

No longer held in insurmountable circumstances

TWO HOURS

+This was an occurrences when as a couple Jill and Johnny

Jill drove 2 hours to get to Johnny their home where he had cooked dunner requiring Jill to clean up after she has worked an 6-8 hours positions so she sat for some minutes got up and wash the before dinner dishes that after sitting quietly holding back tears. Johnny was enduring family members that had expired recently so that night jill cried herself to sleep while johnny slept .the next day / he looked at her waiting to see if she going to do what he had ask dhe looked at him in her mind asking why can he see me being tried from the job. The relationship was developing still in the early stages.

Furthermore the romance starting neither of them knew what was going onthey were both

Staying in their position so continue provide with their family being expecting with the lord God most of items in her ,his, ours they both needing /wanting to endure well

MEN ARE MICROWAVES AND WOMEN ARE CROQUET POTS /Rockets

ROCHELLE KELLY

Thomas Nelson Zondervan Author Affiliation WESTBOW

TWO HOUR

The Jonny, lisa was is married this a when they both are in their daily excepting of one each

Professional Learning creativity. Their involve in her/his lives on with the new positions that have continue once johnny/lisa with accepted each other affirmation commit with life.

They wake up with commitment to each other .= serving each other knowing that purpose was greater than them both. Jill/ Johnny both suffer through the wrestling occurring with God (farher son Holy spirit example is Habakkuk something major good did not show up

 Why God show up? In verse 2 oof the second chapter How long do I have to plead with you about this God I keep asking Why ? why? Why? Why? It cause me to look at iniquity

destructions wickless how long/? How long/? How long?wht was it caught earlier?

The back drop of this is the God bring judgement om the people Babylonian's is captured they Got to make a decision ; strategies for come together couples

1 resign you just do not do anything

2 One thing is detachment going to find something to makr me not to deal with this

3 He men provo hold your chin up g\over rule thing that is crushing

When you disappointed habbakuh 3 chapter 17- 23 bleak reshalt in the Lord I will ejoice the circumstances are out of his control you're weak in 5

Appendix

Each Appendix appears on its own page.

Footnotes

[1]Complete APA style formatting information may be found in the Publication Manual.

Table 1

Type the table text here in italics; start a new page for each table

[Insert table here]

Figure Captions

Figure 1. Caption of figure

[Figures – note that this page does not have the manuscript header and page number]

OVERCOMER

Do not want to wait to get to heaven I want to experience what God has to do in life while here(on earth as it is in heaven. The kind of hot in Texas (laugh out loud slap your mama}

This putting on the beast of [pl;ate of faithful while praying in the sprit with saints (people}. Ephesians6 ;14-18 ,20

Title

Author

Author Affiliation

Abstract

Your abstract should be one paragraph and should not exceed 120 words. It is a summary of the most important elements of your paper. All numbers in the abstract, except those beginning a sentence, should be typed as digits rather than words. To count the number of words in this paragraph, select the paragraph, and on the Tools menu click Word Count.

Title of Paper

Begin your paper with the introduction. The active voice, rather than passive voice, should be used in your writing.

This template is formatted according to APA Style guidelines, with one inch top, bottom, left, and right margins; Times New Roman font in 12 point; double-spaced; aligned flush left; and paragraphs indented 5-7 spaces. The page number appears one inch from the right edge on the first line of each page, excluding the Figures page.

Headings

Use headings and subheadings to organize the sections of your paper. The first heading level is formatted with initial caps and is centered on the page. Do not start a new page for each heading.

Subheading

Subheadings are formatted with italics and are aligned flush left.

Citations

Source material must be documented in the body of the paper by citing the authors and dates of the sources. The full source citation will appear in the list of references that follows the body of the paper. When the names of the authors of a source are part of the formal structure of the sentence, the year of the publication appears in parenthesis following the identification of the authors, for example, Smith (2001). When the authors of a source are not part of the formal structure of the sentence, both the authors and years of publication appear in parentheses, separated by semicolons, for example (Smith and Jones, 2001; Anderson, Charles, & Johnson, 2003). When a source that has three, four, or five authors is cited, all authors are included the first time the source is cited. When that source is cited again, the first author's surname and "et al." are used. See the example in the following paragraph.

Use of this standard APA style "will result in a favorable impression on your instructor" (Smith, 2001). This was affirmed again in 2003 by Professor Anderson (Anderson, Charles & Johnson, 2003).

When a source that has two authors is cited, both authors are cited every time. If there are six or more authors to be cited, use the first author's surname and "et al." the first and each subsequent time it is cited. When a direct quotation is used, always include the author, year, and page number as part of the citation. A quotation of fewer than 40 words should be enclosed in double quotation marks and should be incorporated into the formal structure of the sentence. A longer quote of 40 or more words should appear (without quotes) in block format with each line indented five spaces from the left margin.[1]

References

Anderson, Charles & Johnson (2003). *The impressive psychology paper.* Chicago: Lucerne Publishing.

Smith, M. (2001). Writing a successful paper. *The Trey Research Monthly, 53,* 149-150.

Entries are organized alphabetically by surnames of first authors and are formatted with a hanging indent. Most reference entries have three components:

Authors: Authors are listed in the same order as specified in the source, using surnames and initials. Commas separate all authors. When there are seven or more authors, list the first six and then use "et al." for remaining authors. If no author is identified, the title of the document begins the reference.

Year of Publication: In parenthesis following authors, with a period following the closing parenthesis. If no publication date is identified, use "n.d." in parenthesis following the authors.

Source Reference: Includes title, journal, volume, pages (for journal article) or title, city of publication, publisher (for book).

Appendix

Each Appendix appears on its own page.

Footnotes

[1]Complete APA style formatting information may be found in the Publication Manual.

Table 1

Type the table text here in italics; start a new page for each table

[Insert table here]

Figure Captions

Figure 1. Caption of figure

[Figures – note that this page does not have the manuscript header and page number]

www.ingramcontent.com/pod-product-compliance
Lightning Source LLC ,
Chambersburg PA
CBHW061722120626
46550CB00003B/1327